You and Your Home

UNDER THE MICROSCOPE

You and Your Home

UNDER THE MICROSCOPE

John Woodward & Casey Horton

Blitz Editions

This edition published in 1996 by
Blitz Editions
an imprint of Bookmart Ltd
Registered number 2372865
Trading as Bookmart Ltd
Desford Road
Enderby
Leicester LE9 5AD

ISBN: 1-85605-363-6

Editorial and design: Brown Packaging Books Ltd
255-257 Liverpool Road
London N1 1LX

Printed in Italy

Picture credits
The publishers would like to thank the Science Photo Library for supplying
all of the photographs used in this book, except the following:
page 31: Frank Lane Picture Agency
pages 45, 49, 53: Tony Stone Images

CONTENTS

HAIR TODAY

Our hair is made of a tough, shiny material called keratin. Each hair grows from a root in your skin shaped like a tiny onion. The root adds keratin to the bottom of the hair, and this pushes the rest of it up a tube called the follicle. By the time it reaches the skin surface the hair has become hard and springy, and strong enough to keep growing. The hair on your head usually grows about 12 cm in a year. Each hair falls out after three to five years, so it hardly ever grows more than about 60 cm long.

Looking like sticks surrounded by rose petals, these are hairs sprouting from dry, flaky skin on someone's head. You can see the overlapping scales of keratin.

AMAZING HAIR

- Some people's hair keeps growing longer and longer. The longest hair ever measured belonged to an Indian monk, whose hair was almost 8 metres long!
- A young adult has about 120,000 hairs on his or her head. People with blonde hair have more, while people with very dark or red hair have fewer.

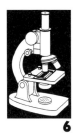

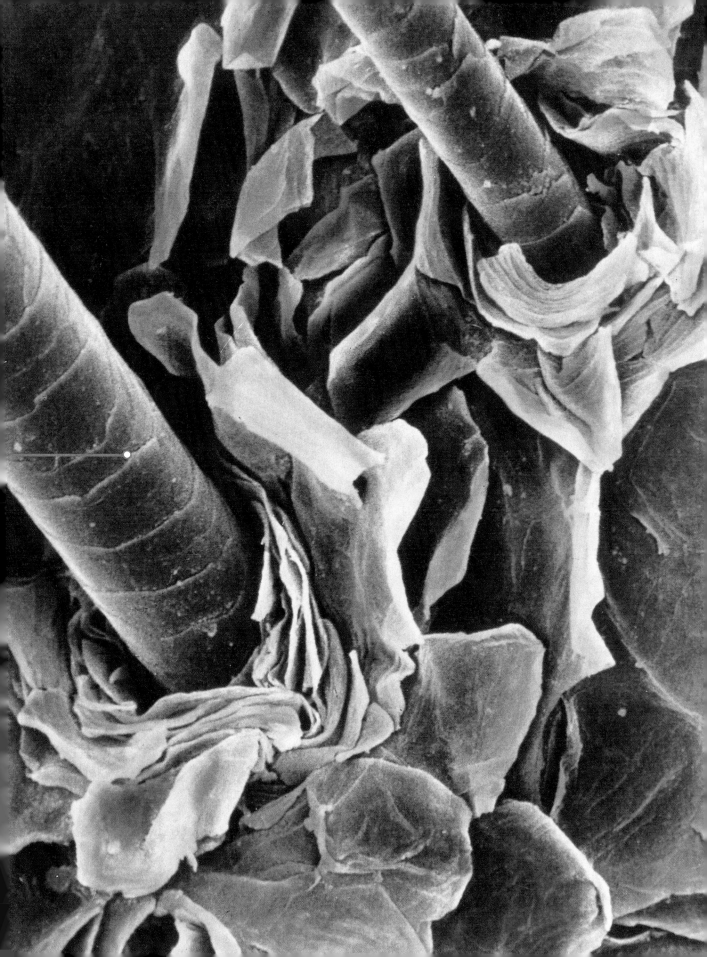

TINY VAMPIRE

Many types of insect feed like tiny vampires, by sucking the blood of bigger animals. One of these is the human head louse, which lives in hair. A louse can walk from one person's hair to another's, so children often catch lice from each other as they play in the schoolyard. Lice can bite, but this doesn't hurt. It just itches. They also lay eggs shaped like little bottles. Each egg is glued to a hair and very difficult to remove. The lice cling on tight, too. The only way to deal with them is to use a fine comb, or poison them with special shampoo.

This blue monster is a tiny head louse, clinging to a human hair with its curved claws. The yellow football is an egg, glued to the hair with strong cement.

LEAVE IT TO THE LOUSE

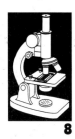

- In one Swedish town, long ago, the mayor was always chosen by getting several men to trail their beards on a table. A louse was then dropped in the middle, and when it crawled into one man's beard he became the next mayor.

SWEATING IT OUT

Our bodies will not work properly if they get too hot, so they have a special way of losing heat. Our skin has little holes all over it called sweat pores. If we become too hot, the pores produce drops of salty water called sweat. The drops lie on the skin surface and gradually turn to steam (evaporate). This uses up some of the heat in the skin below, and cools it down. The system works best in dry air, because if the air is moist the sweat may not turn to steam quickly enough. This is why hot damp weather is more uncomfortable than hot dry weather.

It may look like a crater on the moon, but this is actually a sweat pore on the palm of a man's hand, leading from the gland that produces the sweat.

COOL HEAT

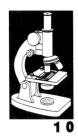

- In very hot countries like Africa and India, people have learned that drinking hot tea and eating spicy food actually helps them cool off. This is because the heat and spice make them sweat a lot. It really works. Try it!

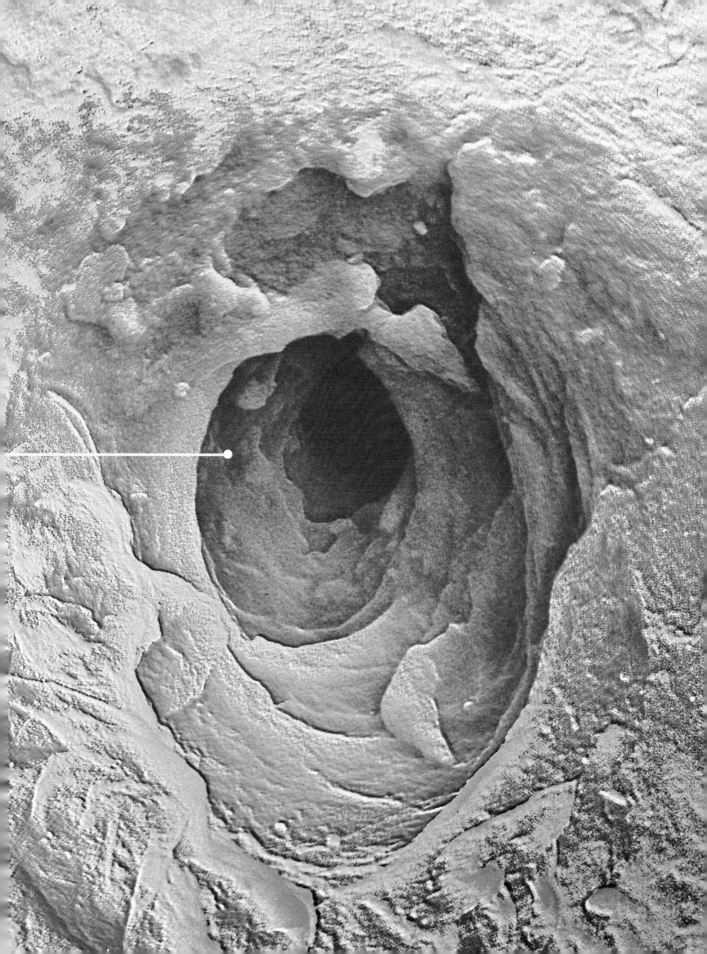

BENEATH THE SKIN

Our skin is very important to our survival. It protects us from infections and stops us drying out in hot weather. It also resists damage, because it has a tough outer coat rather like the bark of a tree. This flakes away all the time, taking dirt and germs with it. Beneath the outer coat lies a thicker layer. This contains the hair roots, sweat glands, tiny blood capillaries and nerves. The nerves are attached to special sensors that detect touch, pain, heat and cold. These sensors occur all over our bodies, but they are most numerous in our fingertips.

In this section through a piece of skin, the tough outer layer is stained red, while part of the inner layer is blue. The large pale ovals are pressure sensors.

DUST CLOUDS

- The tiny flakes that fall from our skin drift around in the air and eventually settle as dust. We each shed about a million of these flakes every 40 minutes, and most of the dust that collects in our houses is actually dead skin.

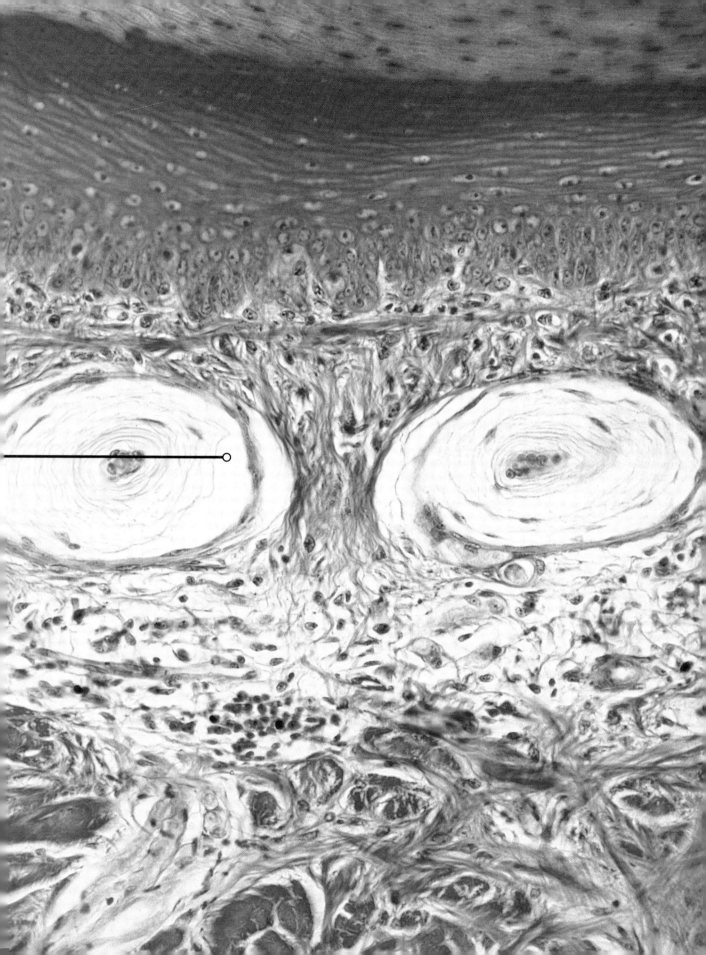

DIFFERENT TASTES

Your tongue has a rough surface because it is covered with hundreds of tiny projections called papillae. The smaller papillae have nerve endings that sense the texture of food. They enable us to feel the difference between smooth and crunchy peanut butter, for example. In between the small projections lie bigger, circular papillae. Each of these has a ring-shaped trough lined with taste buds – special sensors that can tell the difference between sweet, salt, sour and bitter tastes.

Each of the bigger, disc-like papillae on the tongue contains up to 200 taste buds. The smaller papillae between the big discs contain touch-sensitive nerve fibres.

TASTE ZONES

• Each area of the tongue responds to a different taste. Sweet tastes are detected at the tip, salty tastes just behind the tip, sour tastes affect the sides and bitter ones are sensed near the back. If you experiment with sugar, salt and lemon juice, you may be able to sense how your tongue works.

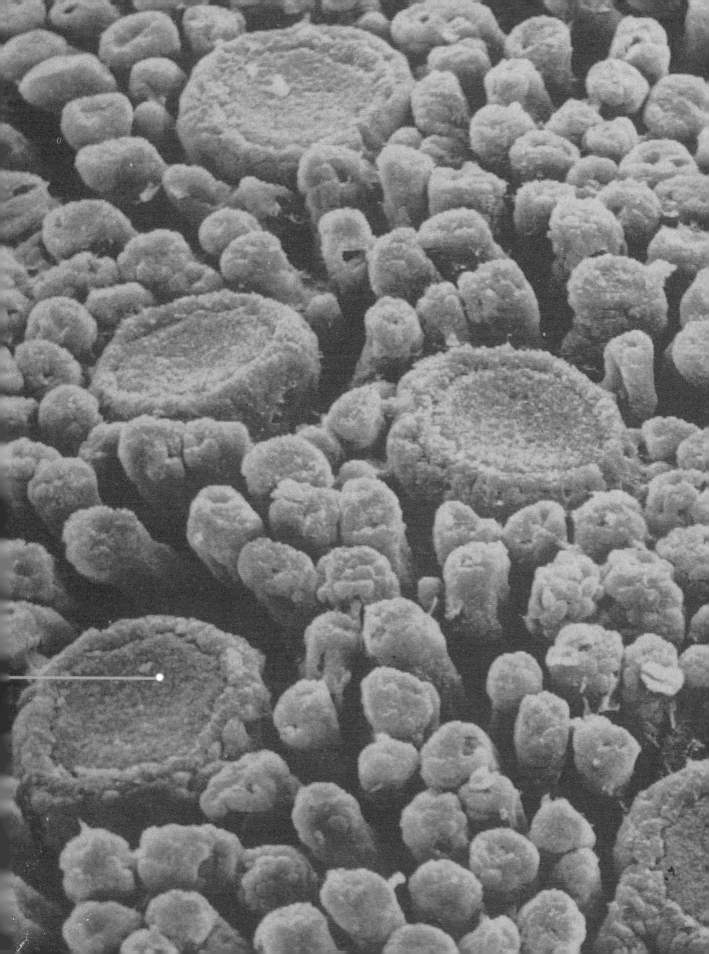

SPONGY BONES

When bones start growing they are completely solid. But as they get bigger they become partly hollow to save weight. The hollow parts are filled with a substance called bone marrow, but they are often strengthened with a bony network of small struts. This makes the inside of a cleaned-out bone look rather like a sponge, so although it is very hard and extremely strong, this type of bone is called spongy bone. The marrow that fills the gaps has the important job of making red blood cells – the tiny red packages that carry oxygen around our bodies.

The network of bracing struts inside a bone keeps it rigid without making it too heavy. The spaces between the struts are normally filled with red bone marrow.

BABY BONES

• A new-born baby has about 350 bones in its tiny body. As it grows up, many of these bones join together, so an adult has only 206 bones. Some of these are very big, like the thigh bone. Others are tiny, like the miniature bones inside our ears.

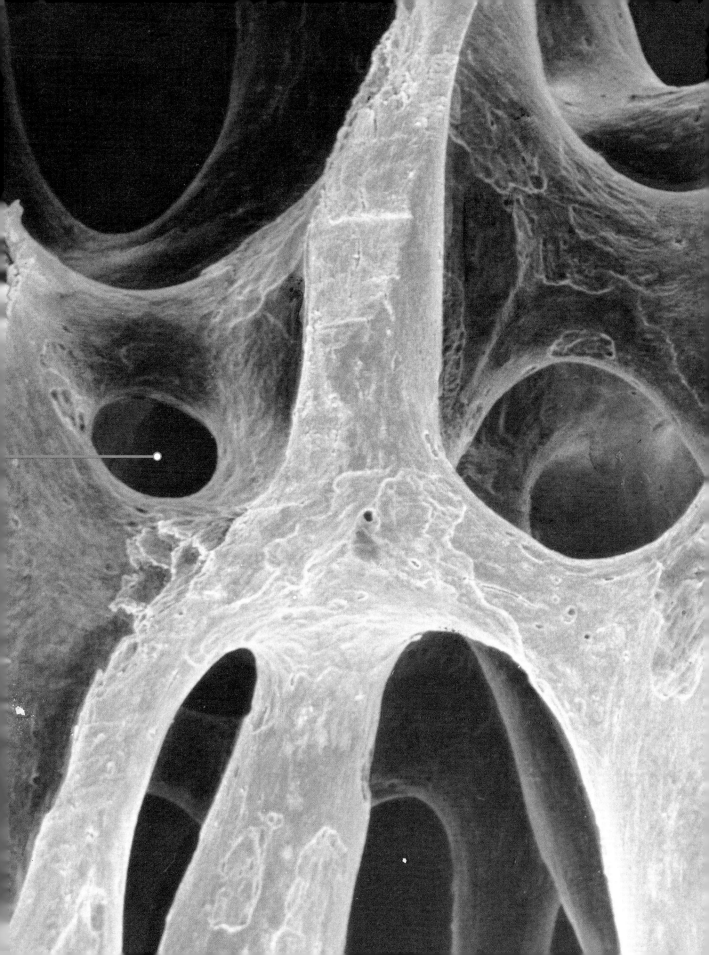

A COMMON COLD

The tiniest flecks of life on earth are called viruses. They cannot survive on their own, so they have to live inside other animals and plants. This means they are parasites, just like lice and tapeworms. But they are so small they can actually live as parasites inside bacteria. Viruses slot themselves into the cells that make up other living things and force them to behave differently. Mostly they make them produce more viruses, but they cause all sorts of other problems. Many diseases are caused by virus infection, including smallpox, the common cold and AIDS.

Magnified 50,000 times by a powerful microscope, a virus looks more like a jewel than a living thing. This virus causes a disease just like the common cold.

VACCINES AGAINST VIRUSES

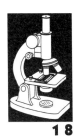

- Virus diseases cannnot be cured easily, because the virus cannot be killed without killing the cells it lives in. But some can be prevented by using vaccines. These make the body kill the attacking virus before it takes over any cells.

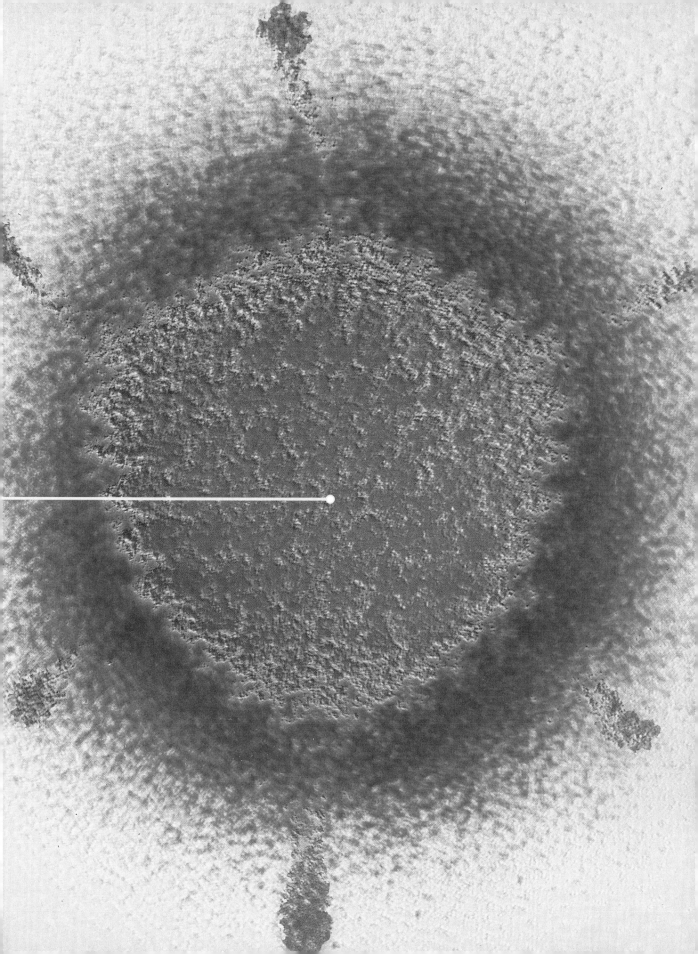

OXYGEN CARRIERS

Just like the engine in a truck, our bodies need fuel to make them work. Trucks run on petrol, but our bodies use glucose – a type of sugar made from food. Our bodies also need oxygen, which they get from the air we breathe. The glucose and oxygen are carried around the body in our blood. The glucose is dissolved in a liquid called blood plasma, while the oxygen is carried by special red blood cells. Tiny tubes called capillaries supply blood to the muscles and other working parts, and these turn the glucose and oxygen into energy.

These red blood cells are charged with oxygen – the gas that muscles turn into energy. When the oxygen is used up the blood returns to the lungs.

BLUE BLOOD

• When blood cells are charged with oxygen they turn bright red. When the oxygen is gone they become dark blue-red. So the colour of blood shows how much oxygen it is carrying. The blood in our wrist veins has very little, so it looks blue.

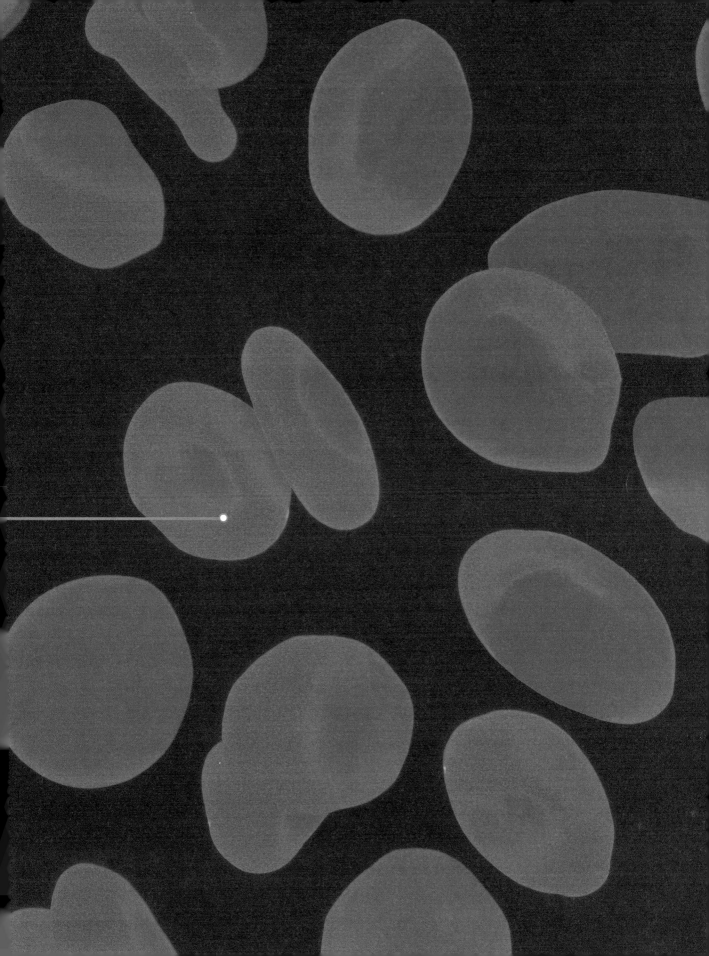

A CLOSE SHAVE

Everyone's hair grows at a rate of about 0.25 mm every day. This may not seem much, and you certainly cannot see how much it has grown each morning. The hair on a man's chin grows at the same rate, though, and if the hair is dark enough you can often see the difference after only a few hours. This means that men who shave usually have to do it every day, and some shave twice daily. The hair is sliced off with a very sharp steel razor or an electric shaver. Before these were invented men used all kinds of things, including the teeth of sharks!

Hairs shaved from a man's chin with a razor blade look like logs of firewood under the microscope. Hair shaved with an electric razor would be torn and ragged.

HAIR-RAISING FACTS

• The longest beard ever measured belonged to a Norwegian called Hans Langseth. When he died in 1927 his beard had grown to over 5 metres long. The beard was preserved and given to the Smithsonian Institute in Washington DC.

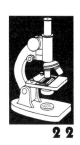

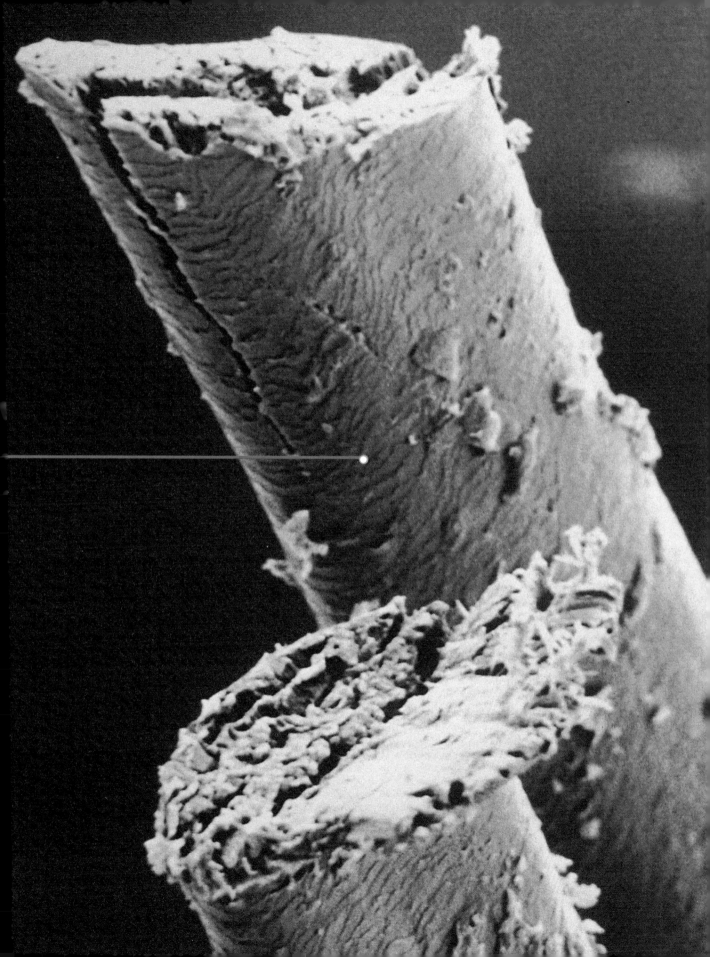

NATURAL BAND-AID

Our blood has a built-in system for sealing wounds. If you cut yourself and blood oozes out, large numbers of tiny cells called platelets glue themselves together to plug the gap. Meanwhile, a liquid protein in the blood, called fibrinogen, is converted into long strands of fibrin. These form a web over the wound, which snares the larger blood cells and creates a clot. Eventually, the mass of cells, fibrin and watery plasma sets into a hard scab. The scab stops bacteria from getting in and causing infection, and enables the wound to heal quickly.

Like fish caught in a net, these red blood cells have been trapped in a web of fibrin to form a clot. This becomes a scab that protects the wound until it heals.

TOO LITTLE, TOO MUCH

- Some people have a condition called haemophilia that prevents their blood clotting, so if they cut themselves they keep bleeding.
- Others suffer from blood clotting inside their bodies, blocking vital arteries.

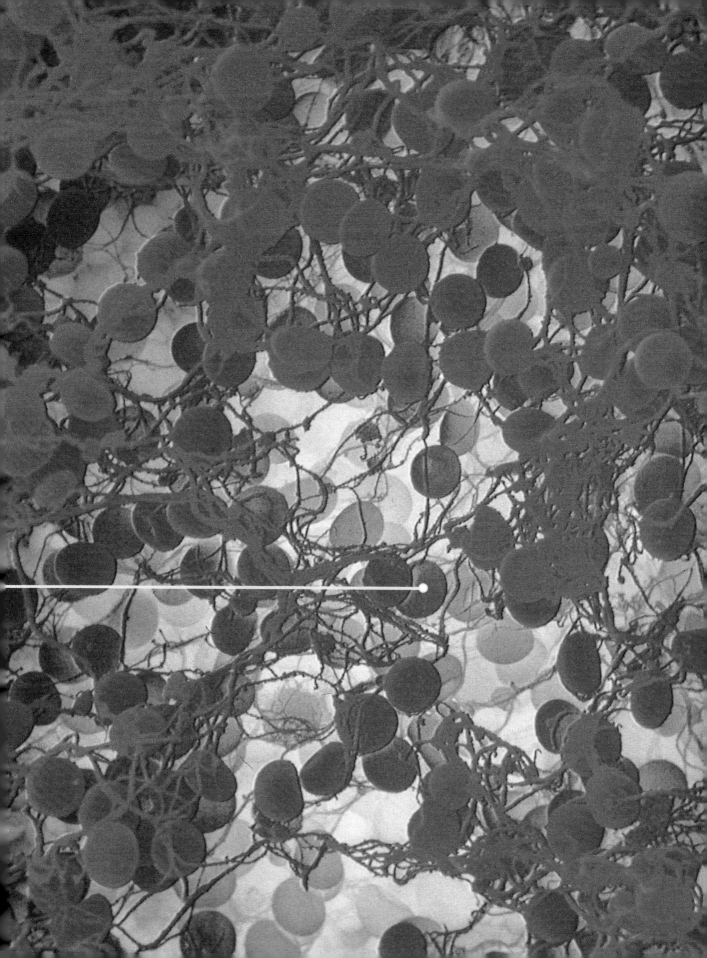

FROM FOOD TO FUEL

Food is no good until it is digested, or broken down into substances that can be used by our bodies. Food is like a complex structure made out of building blocks: if you take it apart, the blocks can be used for something else. In our bodies, the small intestine has the job of taking the blocks apart. It uses substances called enzymes to split the complex foods into simpler products, such as sugars. These are absorbed into the blood-stream through the intestine and carried to the liver. Here they are turned into the glucose that our bodies use as fuel.

The lining of the small intestine is covered in tiny finger-like projections called villi. These make its surface area much bigger, increasing its ability to digest food.

LONG JOB

- From one end to the other, the intestinal tract of a human adult is 10 metres long!
- Most of it is coiled up like a garden hose in the area we call the stomach. The true stomach is higher up, just under your ribs.

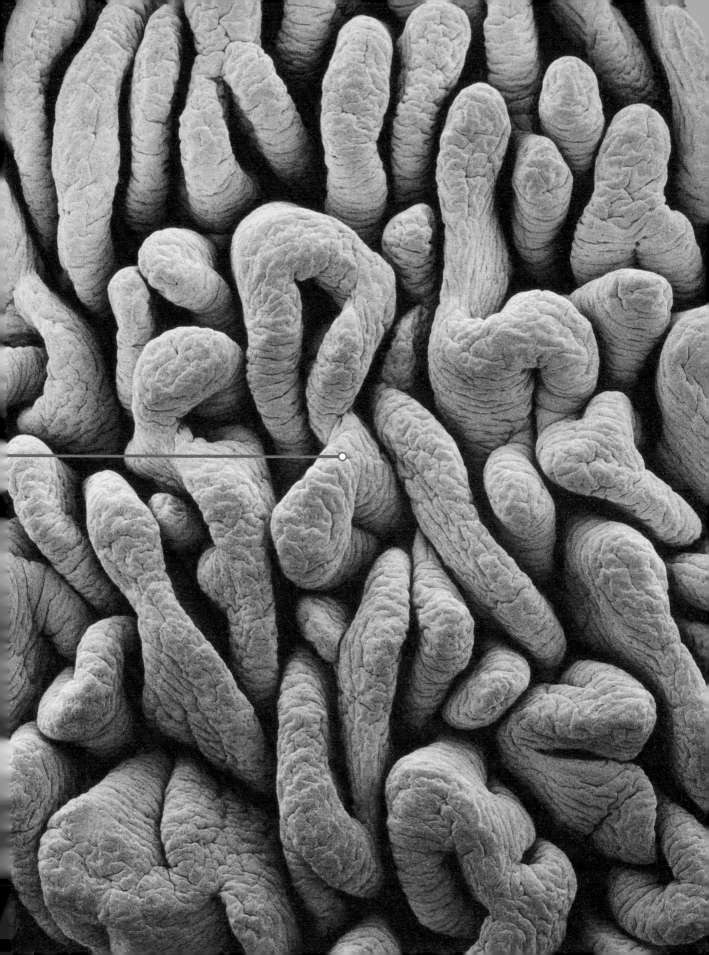

CREATING AN IMAGE

Our eyes are built rather like minia-ture cameras, with lenses that can be focused to form a clear image. The image is projected onto a sheet of light-sensitive cells at the back of each eye, called the retina. There are two kinds of cells: rods and cones. The rods are very sensitive, but they can detect only shades of light and dark, like a black and white movie. The cones are not so sensitive, but they respond to colour. All the information gathered by the cells is sent down the optic nerve to the brain, where the signals are put together to make an image.

There are over 6 million colour-sensitive cone cells (blue) in each eye and 130 million rod cells (pink and purple), which measure levels of light intensity.

NIGHT VISION

• The colour-sensitive cone cells in our eyes do not work in dim light, so as night falls all the colour seems to drain out of our surroundings. We are used to this effect because it happens every night, but it is just like turning down the colour control on a TV.

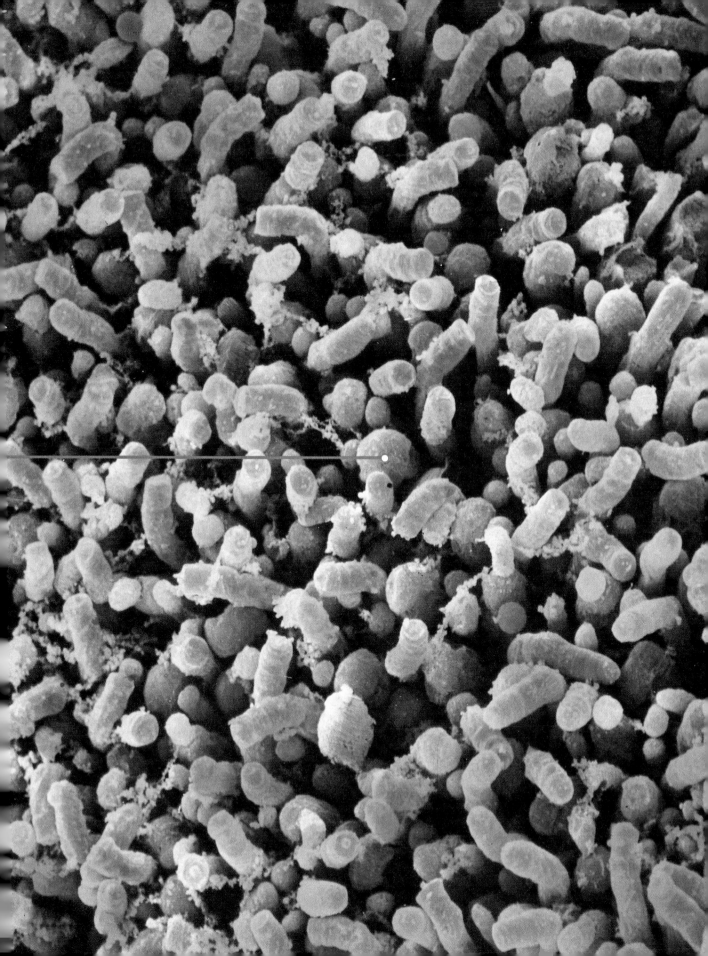

PROCESSING DATA

Our brains are like complicated electronic circuits, wired with electrical nerve cells called neurones. These process information gathered by other nerve cells and send messages to muscles through motor neurones. For example, when you find the sun too bright, the signal travelling from your eyes is analysed in your brain, which then sends a signal to your hand to shade your eyes. But if you are suddenly dazzled, the signal goes directly to your eyelids and makes them blink. This is called a reflex and it happens automatically, without you having to think about it.

This web of nerve cells is part of the natural computer we call the brain. Each cell has a central nucleus fringed with fibres that transmit messages to other cells.

TEST YOUR REFLEXES

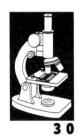

- Cross your right leg over the left and strike it just below the knee cap with the edge of your hand. Your foot will jerk outward.
- Reflexes like this help you react quickly to pain, and avoid severe injuries.

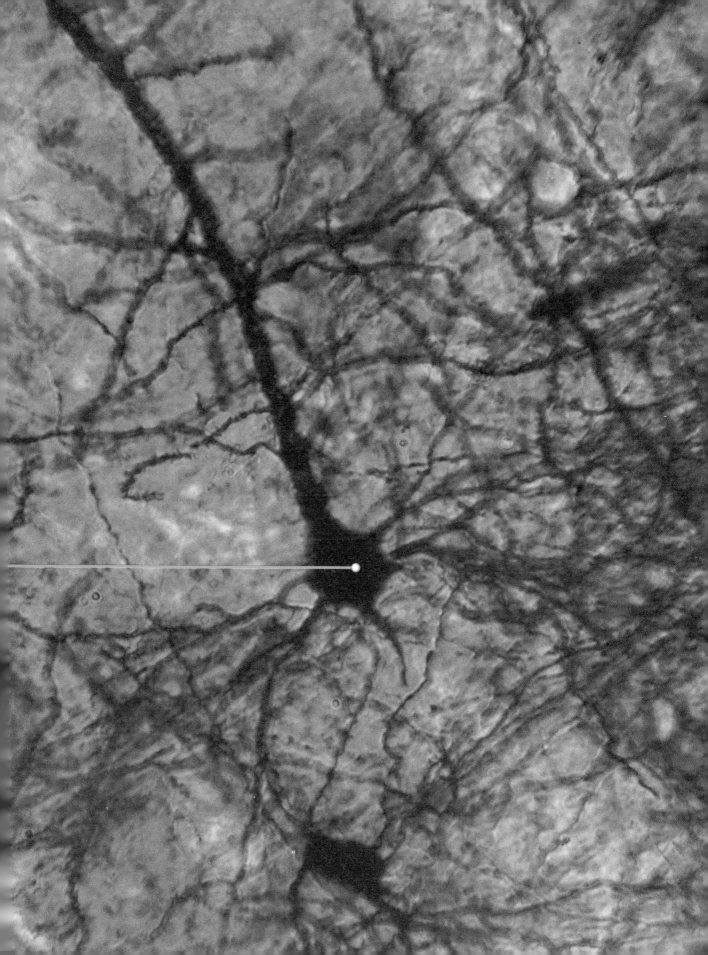

HARMFUL OR HELPFUL

Bacteria are found nearly every-where – in food and water, plants and animals, on the ground and in the air. They are tiny organisms that can be seen only with a microscope. They are 1–10 micrometers long (10,000 micrometers equal 1 cm). Some bacteria are harmful germs that cause diseases such as TB (tuberculosis) and illnesses such as food poisoning. But others are harmless and can be helpful. For example, food manufac-turers use some kinds of bacteria to make yogurt and cheese. Scientists use other kinds of bacteria to make medicines.

The large purple object in this photograph is the head of a pin. The small, yellow objects are bacteria. The picture shows clearly just how tiny bacteria are.

BACTERIA KILLS BACTERIA

• Some bacteria make a special substance that poisons other bacteria. Scientists use these killer bacteria to make medicines called 'antibiotics', such as penicillin. Like other antibiotics it is used to treat diseases caused by harmful bacteria.

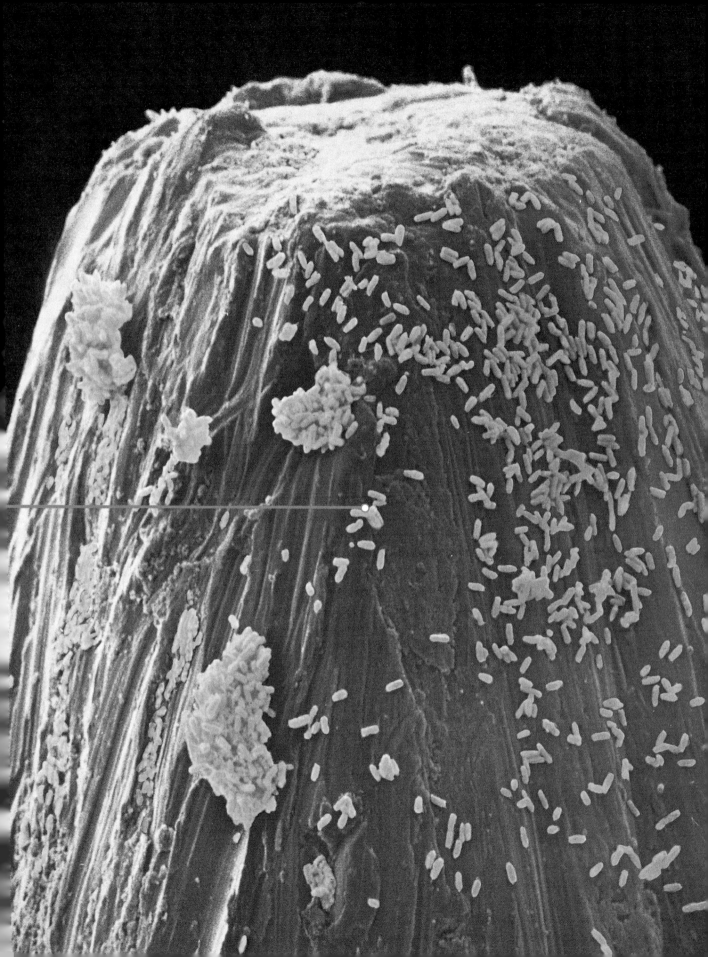

PADDING OUT

Polyurethane is a type of plastic. It can be made into a foam by heating it until it is liquid then blowing gas bubbles into it. Some polyurethane foams are soft and easy to squeeze, like a sponge – in fact, some artificial sponges are made from polyurethane. It is used for stuffing cushions and pillows. Expanded polyurethane is also very useful for keeping hot things hot and cold things cold. It is used in refrigerators and in rocket motors to stop them overheating.

The light areas in this picture are the polyurethane and the darker areas the gas bubbles. The gas bubbles make the polyurethane expand.

FUEL OR PLASTIC?

• Plastic is a man-made material with many uses. A large number of household objects contain or are made from plastic. Most plastics are made from the mineral resources coal, petroleum and natural gas. These materials, which cannot be renewed, are also needed for fuel. As the natural resources run out, who decides what they should be used for?

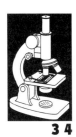

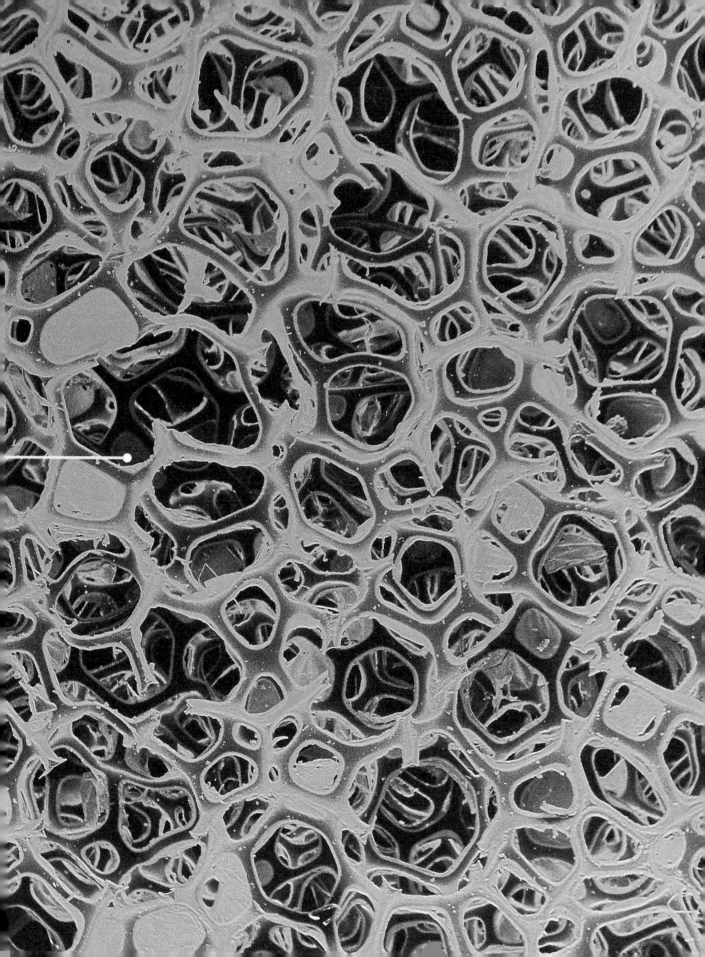

IN THE BAG

Polyester is a man-made fibre made from liquid plastic. The liquid is put into a container that spins around very quickly. As it spins it is forced out through tiny holes in a machine called a spinneret. When the liquid comes through the spinneret it hardens, making a very long fibre known as a filament. The filament is then made into artificial yarns such as polyester. The material known as dacron is the manufacturer's name for a polyester material. The holes in each yarn trap air which keeps in heat and makes it an excellent material for sleeping bags.

These small particles are polyester fibres of dacron inside a sleeping bag. Each fibre has up to seven air spaces which are good for keeping sleeping bodies warm.

EARLY IDEA

• In the 1800s an Englishman, Louis Schwabe, made filaments from molten (liquid) glass by forcing the liquid through fine holes. When the glass liquid came into contact with the cold air the glass hardened into a fibre.

LIGHT INTO SOUND

This compact disc has been broken to show the pits under the clear protective surface. Each of the pits is less than 100th of the thickness of a human hair.

The compact disc (CD) was introduced in 1982. It was designed to record sound. The CD has a base that is sensitive to light. A laser beam is focused on it and the disc is spun around at high speed. As the disc spins, the laser beam is turned on and off to cut pits in the surface. This disc is then used to make copies onto plastic disks coated with a clear plastic layer. The plastic protects the disc. In a CD player the pits either reflect or scatter the light from a laser. The reflected light is changed back into sound. Because there is no physical contact between the laser and the CD, the disc does not wear out.

WHOLESALE INFORMATION

- At present a compact disc can record almost 75 minutes of sound or video or over 100 million words. There are plans to develop discs that can hold many times this amount of information.

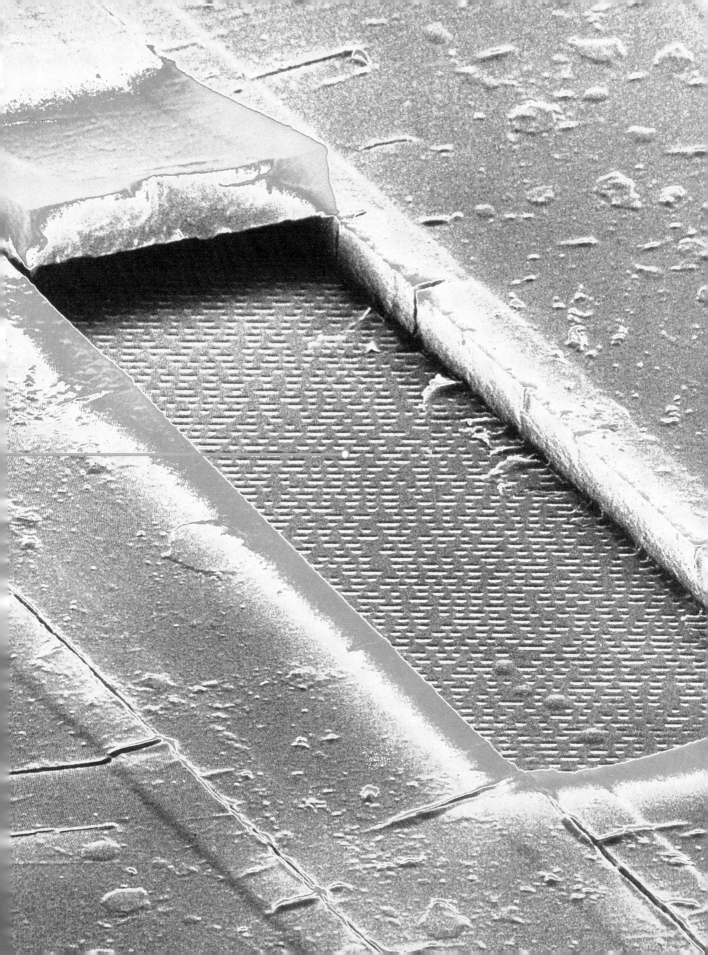

OFF THE HOOK

A Swiss engineer, George de Mestral, invented velcro in 1948. He wanted to know why burrs from plants stuck to clothing and to animal fur. When he looked at the burrs under a microscope he saw that they were made of many tiny hooks. These hooks fastened tightly around fibres of hair and wool. De Mestral used the idea to make the material he called velcro. Velcro often replaces zippers or buttons. Astronauts use velcro in space shuttles to attach objects such as food trays to walls and other surfaces to stop them floating around.

Velcro is made of two strips of material. On one are tiny hooks, on the other are loops. When the strips are pressed together, the hooks grip onto the loops.

MASSES OF HOOKS AND LOOPS

- On a piece of velcro 1 cm square there are more than 700 hooks on one side, and more than 12,000 loops on the other side
- A piece of velcro 6 cm square can support an object weighing up to 450 kg.

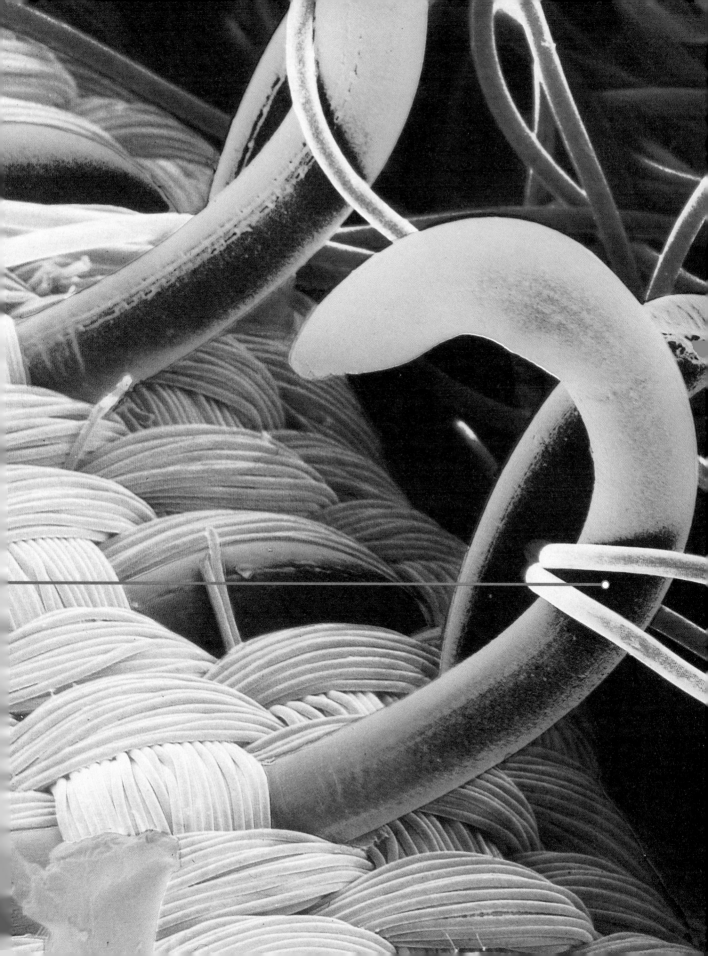

EASY WRITER

Felt-tip pens are markers that are fun, convenient and clean to use. A tube containing a supply of thick ink sits inside the pen holder. One end of the tube is joined to a nib made of natural or man-made felt. This is the writing point of the pen. Ink runs down the tube and flows through the felt tip. As the writer moves the pen across the paper the ink flows onto the writing surface. The ink dries as soon as it reaches the paper. Felt-tip pens can be used for drawing as well as for writing. And some can be used on surfaces such as plastic and glass.

Felt is made simply by pressing wool or synthetic wool fibres together. That is why these fibres are all straight, and not woven together as in other materials.

FIBRE-TIPS

• The nibs of fibre-tip pens are made from bundles of fibres that are held together with glue. They come in different thicknesses, from fine to broad points. Fibre-tip pens last much longer than felt-tips and do not lose their shape.

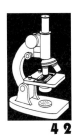

SMALL BUT POWERFUL

Silicon is found in many places and in vast quantities around the world. It is the main material of sand, and is used in the manufacture of glass and electronic equipment known as transistors. Large numbers of transistor circuits can be etched directly onto a wafer of silicon crystal. These transistor circuits are the silicon computer chips that are so important in modern life. Because they are so small they can be used to run many modern machines and instruments, including wrist watches, space probes, computers, calculators, and household appliances such as washing machines and televisions.

This shows part of an integrated circuit on a silicon chip. The large globe is the point of contact to other, external circuits. The connection is made along the gold wire.

MINI COMPUTERS

• In the past, computers were so big that they completely filled a large room. Today, all the parts of a computer can be put into a silicon chip that is no larger than a fingernail.

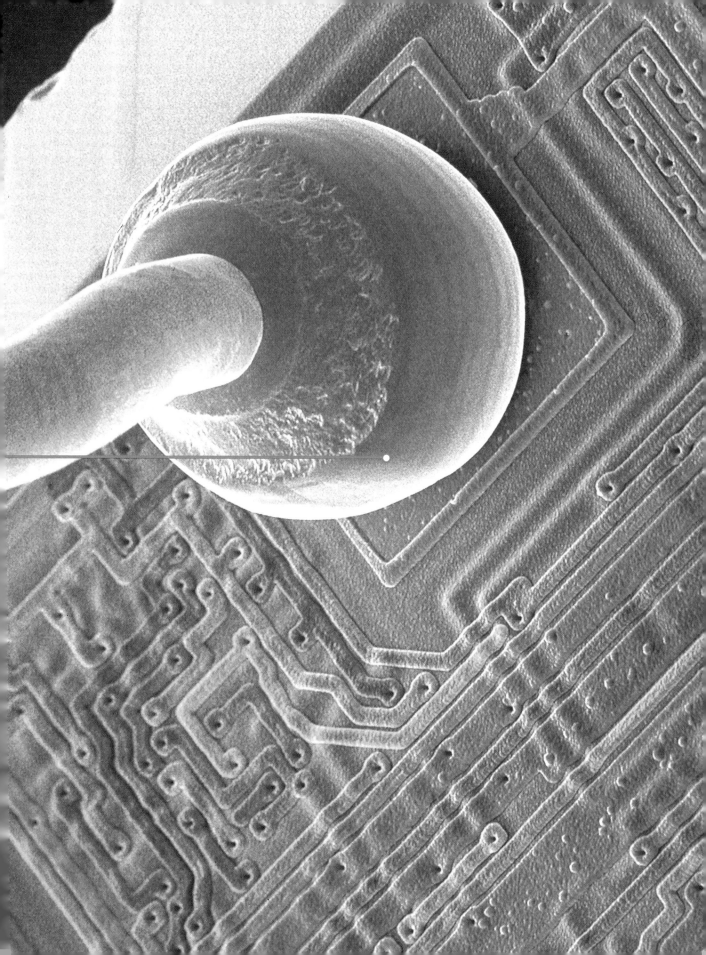

MAKING LIGHT

The part of a light bulb that gives off light is called the filament. It is a very thin wire, only about 0.01 mm thick, and usually made of a metal called tungsten. The filament is attached to thicker wires that run down the glass stem to the bottom of the bulb. When you turn on a light, electricity passes through the tungsten filament and heats it. The filament then becomes so hot that it gives off a bright white light. Light bulbs do not last forever. The heat that makes the bright light slowly weakens the filament and in the end the filament breaks.

The filament in a modern light bulb is made of a very long piece of wire, but it fits neatly inside the glass bulb because it is wound into a tight double coil.

AMAZING HEAT

• Tungsten is a metal that can be heated to a very high temperature without melting. The tungsten filament in a light bulb reaches a temperature of 248°C. Boiling water, which is so hot it will scald your skin, has a temperature of only 100°C.

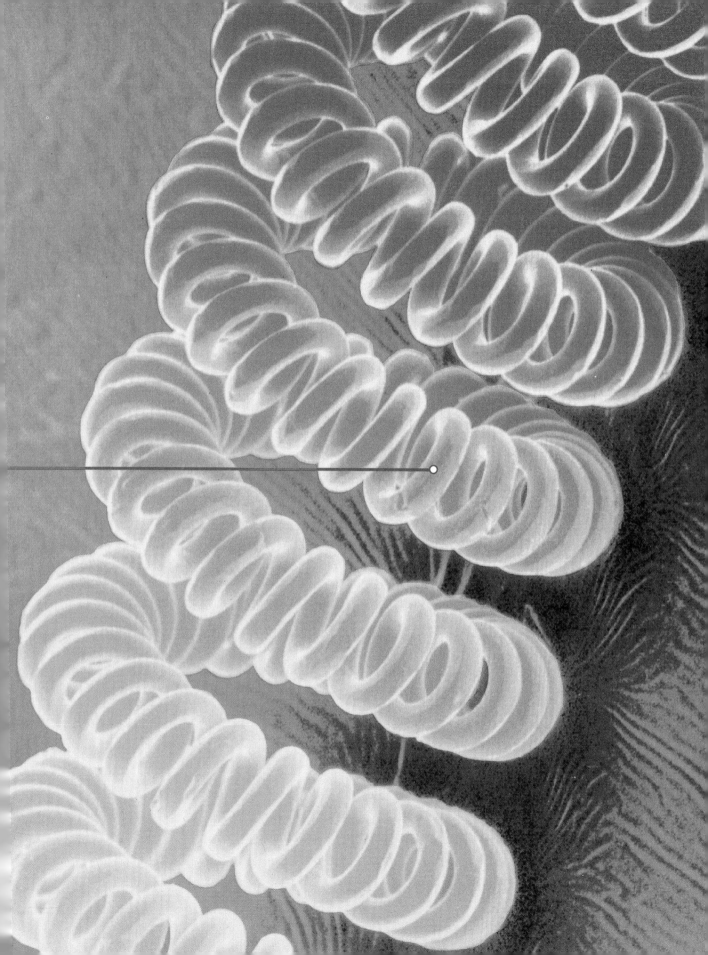

LIFE IN THE DUST

Mites are very small animals that are related to ticks, spiders and scorpions. These creatures may look rather like insects, but in fact they belong to the group of creepy-crawlies called arachnids. Like other arachnids, mites have eight legs and rounded bodies about 0.5 mm long. The dust mite is found everywhere dust is found – in bed-clothes, mattresses, pillows, curtains, carpets, and upholstery. They feed on bits and pieces that make up dust, such as dandruff and flakes of skin. Although they do not directly harm humans, their droppings can cause allergic reactions in many people.

The dust mite has four pairs of legs, two pairs of which are near the front of its head. Also on the front of the head are a pair of fangs and two short limbs similar to legs.

STRANGE HOMES

• Mites live in all kinds of places, including some very odd ones. Some make their homes in the 'ears' of moths, and others live on human skin. The cheese mite lives in decaying cheese.

IRRITATING DUST

House dust is a nuisance to every-one. This unwelcome guest in our homes is a collection of many different plant and animal parts. Much of it is made up of the millions of dead cells that are shed from our skin every day. But hairs – from our own heads and from our pets – tiny insects, and plant material such as pollen also add to the collection. Many of the items found in house dust can cause allergies in some people. Itchy skin and sore eyes are common signs of an allergy, but an allergy can also irritate the airways, causing asthma or other breathing problems.

The large, flesh-coloured object in the centre of the photograph is a flake of human skin. The coloured strands are fibres from clothing and furnishings.

BITS AND PIECES

• As well as human skin, one speck of dust contains an amazing number of other objects, including human hairs. An adult person has about one hundred thousand hairs on their head, and loses between twenty and one hundred hairs every day.

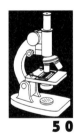

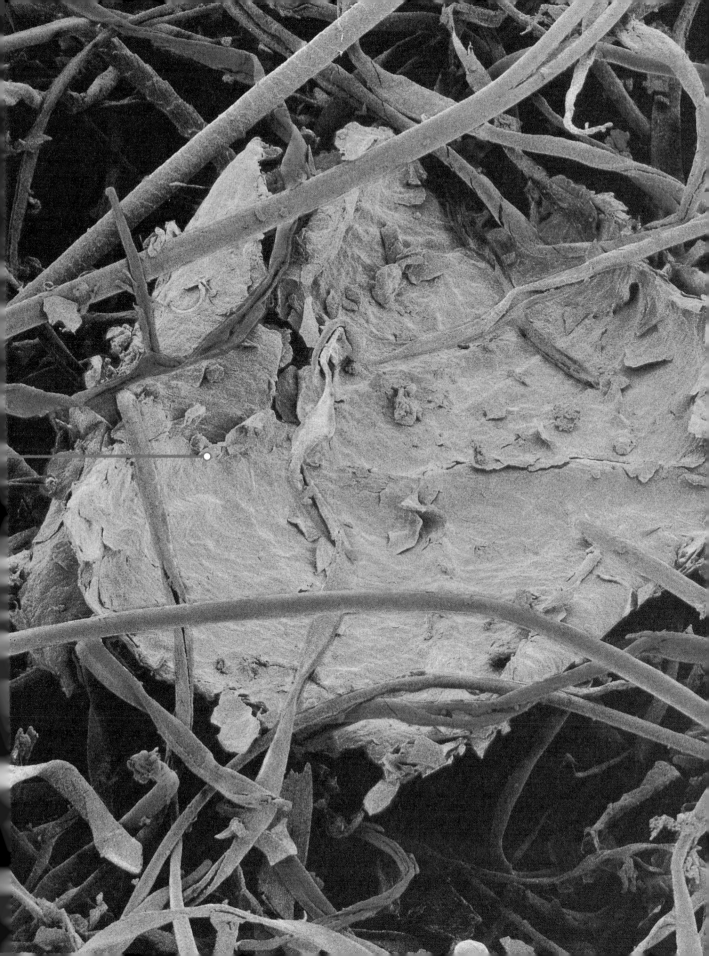

SPINNING YARNS

This picture of cotton shows how the yarns are woven over and under each other to make a piece of material. As the material wears out, some of the fibres become loose and break.

Cotton is a natural material that is used to make cloth. It comes from the cotton plant – a small flowering shrub. As the flowers die they are replaced by round seed cases called bolls. When the bolls are ripe they burst open and form round, creamy-white fluffy balls. This 'fluff' is the cotton. It protects the plant's seeds enclosed inside it. The cotton is separated from the seeds, washed, and pulled into long fibres. The fibres are then spun into cotton yarns by taking several fibres and twisting them together into one long strand.

COTTON BELT

- In Tehucan Valley, Mexico, people have discovered cotton remnants some 7000 years old.
- The USA is one of the world's major cotton-producers. The cotton belt stretches from Florida to North Carolina and west as far as California.

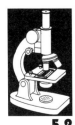

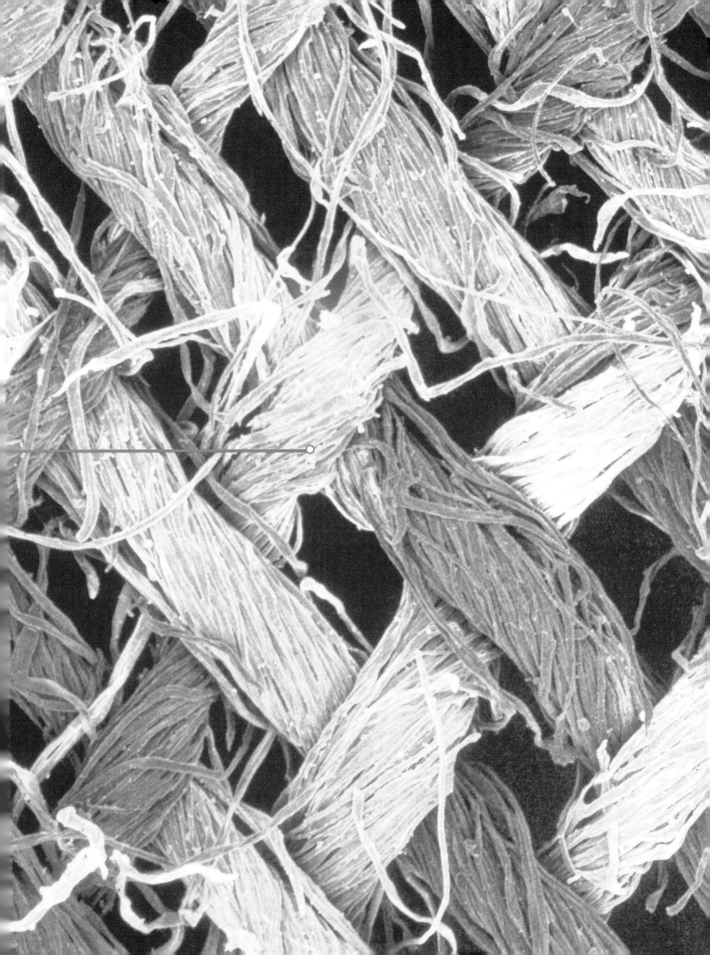

PROTECTIVE COVERING

A sticking plaster may look simple and uncomplicated but it is the result of much research, good design and modern know-how. The pad that covers the wound protects it from further injury and absorbs blood and pus that may seep from the wound. A special covering on the pad stops the pad from sticking to the wound. The plastic film that holds the pad in place is designed to allow the wound and the skin around the wound to breathe. An adhesive coating keeps the sticking plaster in place, but when it is taken off the adhesive does not stay on the skin.

Tiny pores, or openings, in the surface of the sticking plaster allow air to get to the wound. Cuts and grazes heal more quickly if the air can get to them.

FIRST FOR FIRST-AID

- Sticking plasters are an essential part of the household first-aid kit. They should be used to protect minor cuts and other wounds but should never be placed on burns and scalds. Always see your doctor if wounds and burns are serious.

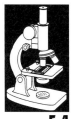

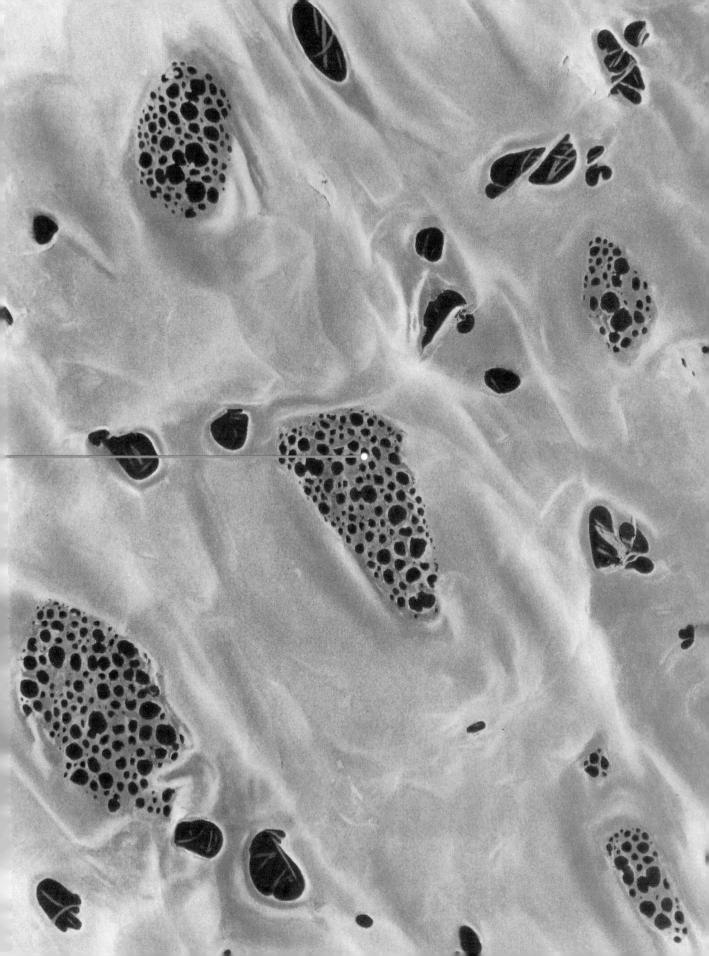

CLIMBING PEST

Cockroaches, like house mice, are common household pests that live in the company of humans and spread disease. They are found in houses and all kinds of other buildings – especially old buildings – where they live on human food and debris. Cockroaches are difficult to capture and kill because they can run at speed and disappear quickly into narrow cracks. The red-brown American cockroach grows up to 4 cm in length. Like other cockroaches it can fly and is an excellent climber.

The spiny front legs of an American cockroach are visible in this photogaph. Like all insects the cockroach has three pairs of legs.

ANCIENT INSECTS

• Cockroaches are among the oldest insects on Earth. Their fossils are found in many places in North America, Europe and the northern parts of Asia. Some of them date back to the Carboniferous Period of Earth's history, which occurred 280 million to 345 million years ago.

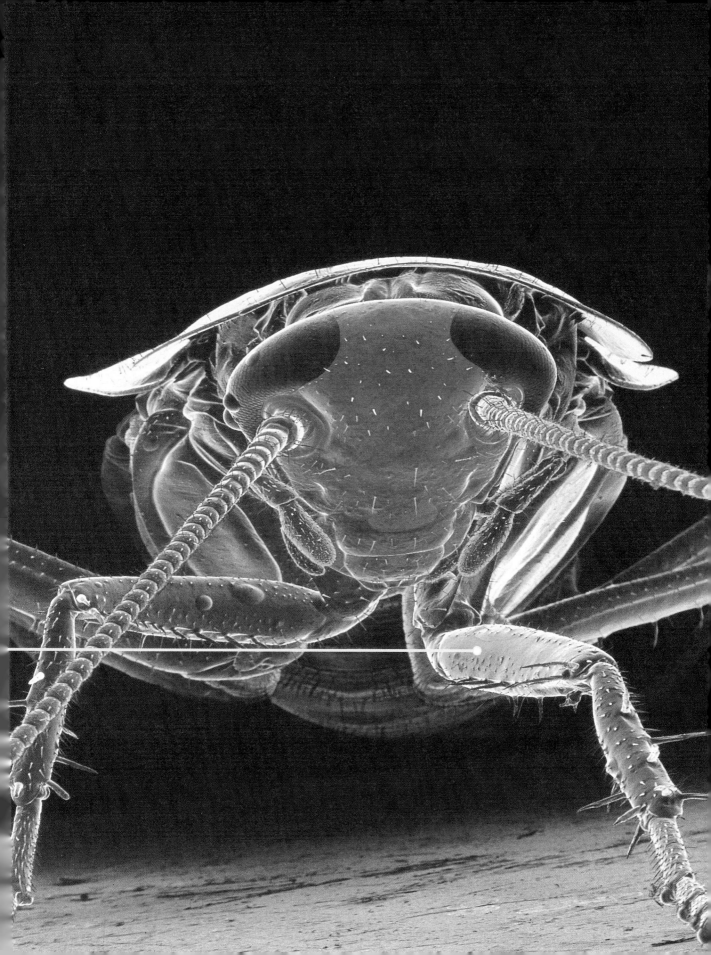

CRISPY SNACK

A potato crisp is just a thin slice of potato, fried in cooking oil. The flesh of a potato is mainly starch. This is a complex mixture of carbon, hydrogen and oxygen, called a carbohydrate. Sugar is made of the same substances, but in a different combination. When we cook potatoes, some of the starch turns into a type of sugar. This is why a cooked potato tastes better than a raw one. By itself, this type of carbohydrate is good food. But when it is soaked in cooking oil and fried to make potato crisps, it becomes very unhealthy.

This potato crisp is smothered in fat, which is lying on the surface like an oil slick. The inside of the crisp is a honeycomb of plant cells, burst by the heat.

PRICE A SLICE

- If you have a food processor in your home, ask an adult to cut a potato into crisp-sized slices. See how many you can get out of one potato. How many potatoes would you need to make a bag of crisps, and how much would they cost?

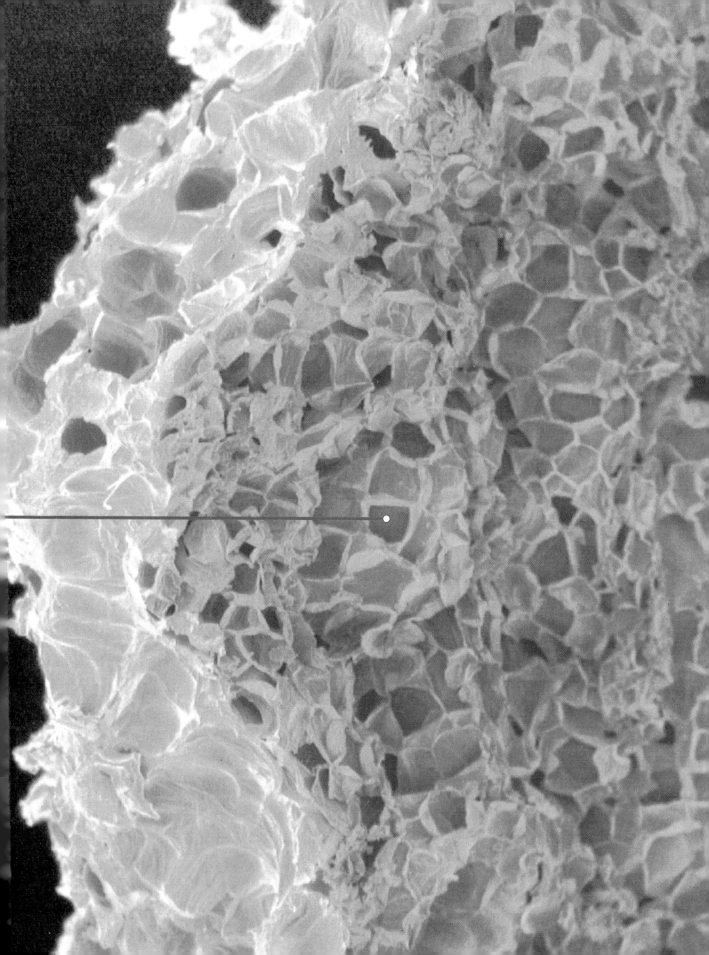

PERFECT CUBES

The salt we use on our food is a mineral called sodium chloride, formed from sodium and chlorine. The tiny particles of sodium and chlorine, called atoms, always link together in the same pattern to make a cube-shaped structure. This cube is the basic sodium chloride molecule. When salt crystals form, their shape echoes the shape of the tiny molecules, so the crystals are cubic too. Pure salt forms perfect cubes, but normally salt crystals come in a variety of more or less cubic shapes. Other minerals form crystals of different shapes, but the principle is the same.

These grains of table salt have had their corners knocked off during processing so the salt pours more easily, but you can still see the cubic structure of the crystals.

CUBE QUEST

• If you use coarse salt in a grinder in your home, check out the crystals with a magnifying glass. Harmless impurities in the salt create all kinds of strange shapes, but if you look for long enough, you may find a near-perfect cube.

LIFE-SAVING MILK

A lot of the food we eat today has been processed in some way. One reason for this is that fresh food doesn't stay fresh. Milk turns sour within a few hours in a hot climate. Dried milk, though, can be kept for many weeks. This makes it extremely useful for emergencies, and a real lifesaver in places where people are starving. Food processing has its downside, though. Most processed foods are not as good for you as fresh foods, and some contain substances that may be harmful. Although processed food can save lives, it is a poor substitute for the real thing.

These milk granules have had the water removed by a quick-drying process, leaving only the solids. These amount to just 13 per cent of the bulk of fresh milk.

MYSTERY FOOD

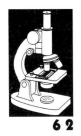

- Get hold of a few food packets and read the lists of ingredients printed on them. Are you sure you want to eat all this stuff?
- The option is to get fresh food and cook it at home. Then you know what you're eating.

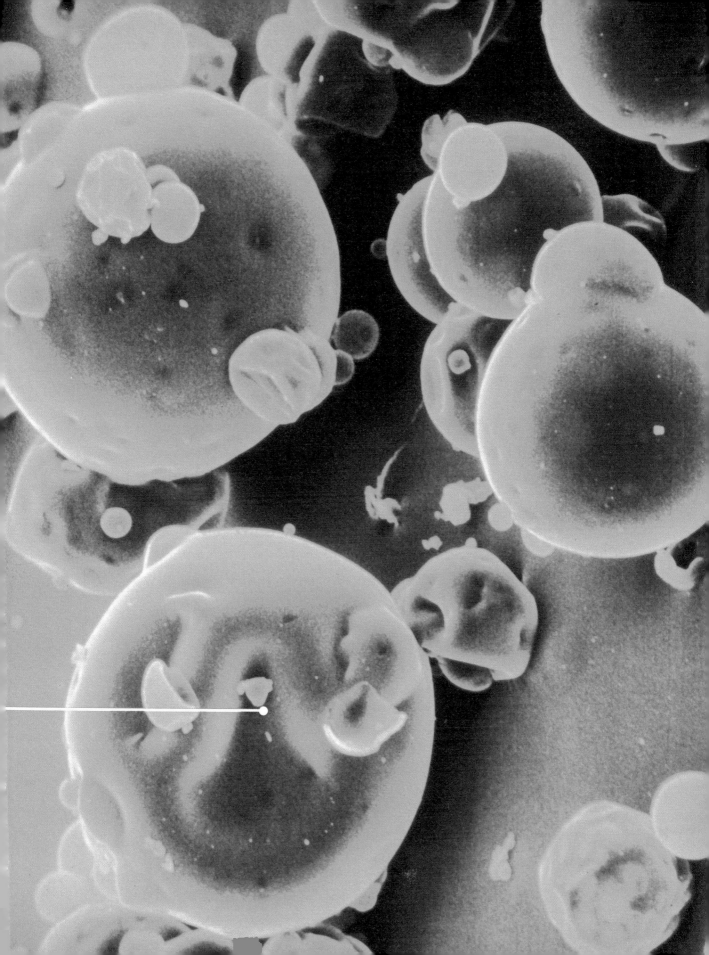

INDEX

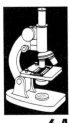